CW00498750

This book is dedica
Ira Kaufman
of the North Star Centre, Boca Raton.
Tthanks for opening the blinds.

Keep the Blinds Open

Keep the blinds open
small child,
let the light in,
dark is in you,
drink the sun,
ride the stallion
to the moon,
romp on craters,
surf the brilliance
in the clouds,
never let on
small child,
that you feed
on scraps.

Forward:

I am an adult survivor of childhood emotional neglect.

A boy who was terribly neglected his entire young life went into a school in Parkland Florida only ten miles from my home and killed seventeen people. My horror and sadness is for the families of those seventeen but also for the neglected young shooter.

Research shows that most violent offenders had childhood trauma, and many were neglected. Childhood neglect also leads to alcoholism, drug addiction, or, as in my case, driven emotionally numb over achievement.

I hope my story will help adults who are suffering in silence and wondering what is wrong with them identify with my journey and seek help, and to enable everyone to understand something of what an emotionally neglected child goes through, and through that understanding perhaps prevent even one child from becoming addicted or violent.

The content is from my journal. I also throw in a poem or haiku every now and then. I write and compose to relieve stress; I write a lot.

Sincerely,

Bett Willett

Opening the blinds:

I had no idea I was emotionally neglected, I had, to be sure, almost raised myself. I was proud of my independence and ability to cope and make do until I couldn't.

We know what happens to us in childhood has an effect upon who we become as adults. The good and the bad: awards, accomplishments, mistreatment or abuse. It all has an impact. But there is something else from childhood which also has an enormous effect it's something that people can't see, it's not what happens to us, it's what doesn't happen, it's emotional neglect.
Emotional neglect is not a deliberate act of physical or sexual harm which is what we normally think of as child abuse. Emotional neglect is called invisible because the children are usually not bruised or battered, they are often physically well cared for.

Emotional Neglect is a parent's failure to act. It's a failure to notice, attend to, or respond enough to a child's feelings. Neglect sometimes occurs in circumstances that place families under extraordinary stress for example, death, divorce, illness or disability but also occurs in seemingly happy families, those which have no depth of connection or emotional intimacy. It's not visible or noticeable it is insidious and overlooked while it does its silent damage to people's lives. People who grew up neglected may not even realize that their struggles could be connected to childhood emotional neglect.

They have difficulty knowing and trusting their own feelings as well as others' because their emotions were not validated as children. Because their emotional self has been denied, they may find themselves feeling disconnected, unfulfilled or empty. Traumatized children often have

3

distressing memories of their past which are so painful that they completely repress them.
They may have difficulty trusting or relying on others.
They may have depression. Many describe feeling that they are different from other people; as if something is wrong with them, but they're not sure what it is, they feel confused and blame themselves for not being happier.

Some Adult Symptoms of Childhood Trauma and Emotional Neglect.

1. ***Anger to yourself can result in:*** *Eating disorders, depression, substance abuse and or Alcoholism, learning problems, promiscuity, choosing the wrong partners, and trying to continually please.*
2. ***Anger focused outward can lead to****: Theft, vandalism, fighting, needing to be in control.*
3. ***Reactions:*** *Being in a constant fight or flight mode, inability to see others' motives, especially romantically. Constantly seeks validation by working to achieve positions of power and or control, becoming an adrenalin addict. Many go into the helping professions, teacher or therapists, etc.*
4. ***Withdrawal:*** *In a relationship there is a constant fear of rejection and if criticism or non-acceptance is felt, walls go up as a defense.*
5. ***Future thinking:*** *Every action is planned, all possible eventualities, mostly the worst, are considered, small problems are often cast as possible disasters.*
6. ***Attracting the wrong partner:*** *The inclination to attract people who are controlling narcissistic, antisocial types.*

7. *Misinterpretation:* Not seeing what was done was trauma or abuse, excusing people and blaming yourself for what was not in your control or your fault.
8. *Depression:* many with C-PTSD spend their life with depression and frequently have major episodes.
9. *Fear of Rejection–* a constant belief that people will abandon or reject you, irrational but constant.
10. *Second Guessing* – Constantly questioning what others think, say and do.
11. *Self-Image* – a negatively skewed perception of strengths and weaknesses.
12. *Low Self-Esteem* – having a negative opinion of one's self not based on reality.
13. *Anxiety and Panic -* episodes of fear or anxiety with physical reactions, often immobilizing.
14. *Need to be Perfect* – to avoid criticism the need to do things perfectly is all out of proportion to reality.
15. *Amnesia* – Repressing events and falsely remembering events as a coping mechanism.

I found a therapist when my marriage was in trouble because my husband was an alcoholic and after many years of heavy drinking was now passing out every day and I was at my wits end.

I needed help, or validation, or something like that, I wasn't sure. What I did know was that I couldn't deal with my life by myself anymore. I was very close to a complete breakdown. I checked the internet for a therapist near me and got lucky when I found Ira.

I saw Ira alone for the first couple of visits. His center has a waiting room with three doors leading to therapy rooms.

Ira's room has a brown leather chair and sofa; he sits in a leather chair with a hassock foot rest next to a desk. My first decision was whether to sit in the chair or on the sofa. As I walked in that's all I could think about, where should I sit, as I only had about four seconds to decide I chose the sofa which was directly across from his chair.

Ira is ruggedly handsome with a mustache and small beard, medium tall and of average weight. He had on a light gray suit and tie which he wore easily but I had the distinct feeling that he would rather be in jeans. The room is softly lit and has big windows overlooking trees and a stream. I told him I needed help to get my husband Jim to quit drinking and I don't know how to do that. I didn't know what to expect as the only other time I had seen a therapist was for a very short time during my first divorce.

Jim's a really nice guy, I said. He is caring and a good person, I said. And, he is making me crazy. Ira asked lots of questions, and I said, yes he drinks every day, yes he is drunk almost every evening, yes he starts drinking about two o'clock, and yes he passes out at the dinner table too many times a week.

Ira asked a lot of questions about Jim, but he seemed more concerned with me and how I was feeling. That was quite refreshing to me, I was there for Jim and his problem, but here this guy was interested in how I was handling life. Something I usually gave very little thought to.

I was single-mindedly focused on how to get Jim to stop drinking, I wanted Ira to talk to him and convince him that he was better off sober, and make him quit. Even Ira's warning about how fewer than ten percent of people Jim's age were successful, didn't frighten me.

Ira was so understanding and supportive that I was certain he was the magician who could wave his wand and give me a sober husband. Ira kept asking me how I felt when I had to make excuses for Jim and spend every evening alone after Jim passed out. I wasn't there for me so as nice as it was to have someone care about my feelings, I concentrated on Jim.

This was our second marriage; before we retired we had both been teachers in the same school district. The story about how we met was a fun one we both loved to tell to unsuspecting victims. We always started the story off by saying that I married my secretary, which was always met with puzzled laughter. I was the newly elected president of the local teachers' association, and Jim, who I had never met, was the newly elected secretary. At the first executive board meeting there was no Jim. I asked our mutual friend, the treasurer, Rich where he was and found out he was a soccer coach and that I wouldn't see him until after the last game in late November. Jim loved telling this story adding how annoyed I was but that I had grudgingly to admit that the meeting minutes were always finished and sent to the board on time, a substitute was dragooned into attending the meetings and giving Jim the minutes notes. I finally met him in December, and the new board, involved in late night salary negotiations and contract provisions soon became close friends.

After a couple of meetings with Ira alone, I brought Jim in. Ira dragged answers out of Jim about his background and his childhood, talked about why he drank. "I like bourbon", he said. Sitting on the sofa quietly as I could, while I was yelling at myself in my head, "Don't interrupt, don't clarify, let him answer himself." Jim is a quiet person, and he kept shooting me puzzled looks, as if I should jump in and answer Ira for him, after all I was the one who wanted to be there, and I dragged him in.

We saw Ira two more times together; Jim cut down on hard liquor and was trying to stay to beer and wine. Anyone who has lived with a substance abuser could have told me what was coming next, but I wasn't hearing any of it. Ira said rehab was the best way to make sure Jim quit entirely. I pushed Jim into agreeing to go.

The rehab residence was a twenty eight day program, I called two before finding one on that would take Medicare and had good reviews. I talked to one of the counsellors. He was very kind on the phone, my questions must have been old to him, but he was sympathetic and of-coursed all my concerns. He said they could take him today and a car would pick him up. Whoa, I thought, today? Oh my god, what have I done? But Jim agreed and off he went. I was alone in the house.

Der mentsh trakht un Got lakht

I wonder what the gentle manatees
meandering up the Intracoastal
munching seaweed think
when reckless speedboats smack into them?
Do they moo "Oh, crap"?
Do they also wonder what they have done to offend?

At my next visit to Ira he was incredulous that Jim agreed to go to the rehab program, he said maybe Jim would be one of the successes. Ira was being optimistic, at least to me. I am pretty sure he had some major doubts.

Rehab was a failure. Jim didn't last the whole 28 days; he checked himself out in a week. He chose alcohol over me and we started to work out our separation then divorce. I then saw Ira by myself and he really zeroed in on me and my feelings and my unusual childhood. I said I felt I was losing myself and didn't know if I was a person anymore or just a reactive blob.

Right there Ira laughed out loud; it's a really happy laugh, and good to hear. The laugh also calmed me down and evened out some of the fear I had as I was trying to figure out what was going on and what he was trying to get me to understand.

He had already helped me understand that I didn't have to be in control of what happened to Jim and I didn't have to fix it. This was a big jolt; I have always been the "fixer". Just realizing that this was not something I had to do all by myself was a big load off of my mind and my anxiety really abated.

It took a lot more convincing by Ira to get me to realize that I was always the "other woman" to Jim, his first love was his Jim Beam and that I should have no guilt about him.

What I am going to tell you now took Ira many months to get me to admit, months and months, because of the shame I felt I wouldn't trust him and didn't feel safe telling him about my past for a long time. I felt really guilty about my childhood and how I failed my family and I wasn't going to let anyone, even this kind and understanding therapist, know what a mess I was.

Memories

What I hate about the canyon is the echo
it's not a grand canyon
but it's very deep.

Many of the layers along the walls
are blunted and faded,
others have jutting sharp outcroppings,
the colors near the bottom
are muddy and murky.

My shouts rappel erratically,
caroming off of crumbling fragments
plummeting through the past
spurning soft ledges
for granite surfaces sealed for centuries,
causing cracks and leaks
before reverberating back to the rim.

After I finally, in bits and pieces, told Ira about my childhood, it took even longer for him to get me to realize I was not at fault for the failings of the adults in my life. That was an enormous breakthrough, and makes my writing this possible. I had no idea what my being neglected and traumatized as a child did to me.

No Cape

In a small canal fronting building
there's a nice office, leather, soft lighting.
Camouflage surroundings for a super
hero who shoots lightning on demand.

As super heroes go, he is unique,
sure he has the usual special super hero car
and a really good daytime disguise
but no cape, he refuses to wear one.
He says he doesn't have to advertise
his super powers, people who need them,
sort of like following the bat signal
in reverse, find him.

When he unleashes his frightening
lightning against the demon du jour
it first struggles then sizzles and bursts
in a sad powerless weak breeze.

Often he has to cauterize
the bloody demon wounds, an ugly
process, but effective, with some scarring.
At times he only has to brighten a path
for the lost in the dark.

It's awesome to see the flash of righteous anger
before he releases his explosive bolt.

I grew up in the suburbs. We lived in a house on a short street lined with big old colonial houses. Our house, which I shared with my older brother, Danny, little sister Marion, and my mom and dad, was set on a 50' by 100' lot. It had a big roofed front porch and a struggling lawn, which had all but given up. There was a worn a dirt path from each corner of the yard across to the porch steps, no kid in the neighborhood, it seemed, had the patience to last 15 more feet to get the front sidewalk every one of the forty or so children in our three-block playing range cut across the lawn, every one, every time, so my father gave up and just mowed what was left.

My brother was born three or four years after my mother lost twin boys in her eighth month of pregnancy. She was unsure she would ever have more children, when my brother Daniel came along a beautiful blond green eyed cherub; she was ecstatic, there are two albums of pictures of his baby years. Five years later I made my appearance, and three and a half years on my accidental sister Marion surprised everyone. Squeezed between an older favored brother and a cute chubby blond baby sister I was kind of overlooked. There are a few pictures of me; most of them have Danny or Marion in them also.

The "Middle Child Syndrome" is very real. Middle kids are often ignored and grow resentful of all the parental attention given to the oldest and the baby of the family, and feel short-changed. Middle children have to try harder to "be heard" to get noticed.

We had no TV until I was ten years old. Parent involvement in our games was nonexistent. We were on our own to fill our time after school and summers.

In Elementary school my mother saw no reason to get involved with what was going on in that was our business.

I was in a second grade brownie troop. When I got to school all the other girls had on their brownie uniforms but I had forgotten it was brownie day. I remember how I felt when I snuck down the stairs of the school and ran home skipping brownies that day. Mothers are supposed to keep track of things like that, aren't they? I made sure I did for my kids.

As kids, during the everlasting summers we were outside from morning until bedtime with brief visits home for food. We roamed the town and woods nearby. We played on our street for hours with no cars to worry us.

Some days I might join a baseball game in an empty lot, then play canasta with my friends Dickey, Suzanne and their little brother Phillip, we taught him to play even though he was only five because we needed a fourth player. I might spend some time weaving potholders out of cotton loops to sell for candy money and then ride my bike downtown to the library. I was working on reading all the books in the children's department in order, from the left side of the top shelf to the bottom right of the last shelf. I never made it, but I spent hours living magnificent adventures and exploring alien countries and planets. I might wind up, after dinner, playing flashlight tag or spot back in the empty lot until bedtime.

Mr. Woodruff was one of our neighbors, he dove a big pickup truck with high wood slat sides. He always dressed the same in a long sleeved tan cotton work shirt with the sleeves rolled up, webbed belt with a shiny brass buckle, brown suspenders stretched over his round stomach, tan cotton work pants that were a little too short and showed white socks above his black hard toed work shoes. He had brownish-gray brush cut hair and he always needed a shave. I wondered at that. How could he always need a shave? If he didn't shave at all he would grow a beard so he must have shaved sometimes but I never once saw him clean-shaven. It was a mystery.

Dickey, Gail, Sue, pain in the neck Harold and I were Mr. Woodruff's helpers. He called us his sidekicks. He worked for the post office. One of his jobs was picking up sacks of mail from the train station. He needed us to help him move the sacks of mail from the train platform to the truck and then to the back platform of the post office.

On the days we helped him, we were out of the house extra early. Whoever was ready first ran to pick up the others. We never, rang doorbells or knocked on doors. The neighborhood etiquette required a loud shout outside the lowest window. The words never varied, only the name used. "HEY DICKEY, CAN YOU COME OUT AND PLAY"? We would then run down our street, to wait for Mr. Woodruff, and his truck, in front of his sister's big dark brown house where he lived. Sue had to cut through the backyards from the Boulevard. We road to the station in the back of the truck, Mr. Woodruff stopped to pick up my best friend Gail further up the avenue. None of us wanted to ride up front but we knew Mr. Woodruff needed company so one of us would reluctantly join him. We supposedly took turns sitting with Mr. Woodruff, but we stuck Harold with it more often than not.

We rode to the train station waving and yelling to everyone we knew along the way. We turned on South Avenue, under the then bare-of-graffiti railroad bridge, past the firehouse, waving to the firemen polishing the hook and ladder in the rear and wound up next to the train platform where canvas sacks of mail awaited us. We helped pile the sacks in the truck. Mr. Woodruff wanted them in just so, big ones first. Sometimes he would trip over one of us and we would erupt in peals of mocking laughter at the unfortunate victim. Another important aspect of our job began then. We had to sit on the sacks and make sure they didn't fall off the truck. Back we went, past the firehouse again to the post office loading dock where we unloaded. Mr. Woodruff had to stay at the post office so we made our own way home, trying to ditch Harold somewhere along the way.

In addition to Mr. Woodruff there were a lot of adults who needed our help doing their jobs. They included most of the firemen, Albert the policeman, Joe the butcher, Mr. and Mrs. Wadell in the delicatessen and, the high school students in the snack stand at the football games where I first tasted coffee.

I was overly shy around adults and a hyper sensitive child. Ira diagnosed Attention Deficit Disorder as well as Post Traumatic Stress Disorder, but as a child, what I knew was that everyone else seemed to be able to do and handle things so much better than I and I was constantly wary of making mistakes.

My parents were not much involved with what we did as kids even before my mother got sick, we were fed and clothed, but not fussed over. Telling Ira about my early education I realized that starting on day one, I had not only no support, but in many cases had active disapproval from teachers the whole thirteen years.

When I was four years old and in kindergarten I hurried into the classroom, I could hardly wait for what was coming. Yesterday, our first day of school, I knew every song and I thought that maybe today we would have something new. Before she went to the piano the teacher leaned over me and said, "Don't sing out loud today, just move your mouth." I remember the embarrassment to this day; the rest of the year with this judgmental witch was misery. Decades later I, told my students that my kindergarten teacher helped make me the teacher I was.

My third grade teacher was having some kind of breakdown and retired after our year, but that was too late for me, her wild accusations against those of us who weren't her pets made learning anything from her impossible. She said I had better not act like my brother, that my handwriting was lousy just like his, but at least he could do arithmetic, why couldn't I?

Of course the message I clearly received was that I wasn't smart enough. No one realized that because of the stress of being neglected at home and the added stress of having a crazy teacher I couldn't concentrate at all.

I learned, but not what they wanted me to. I learned I was dumb, I learned to be quiet, I learned to hide my defects and my feelings, I learned to stay far away from adults, I learned that no one had my back, I was all alone, I also learned the futility of trying.

Splinters

I climbed over the fence
past the no trespassing sign
with no fear that I would be stopped.
No one had cared about this stretch
of beach for years,
not since the disaster.

I carefully lifted my flip flops
and stepped around
the twisted boardwalk splinters
knowing if I tripped
I would have to pick painful slivers
out of my knees.

I thought about this morning.
I don't know what possessed me,
what made me blow off my obligations,
pull on my shorts and get into the car.

I drove obsessed, with no control
over where we were going
and only found out
when we created a space
among the weeds and parked.

My ten year old self
ran up the parking lot ramp
barefooted, darted
across the boardwalk
to the beach stairs
and danced over the sandy
griddle to the water's edge.

I watched, riveted.

I breathed her joyful breaths,
and goosebumps appeared
on my arms as she dived
ecstatically into the waves.

With blurring eyes
I blindly groped my way
closer to the railing
trembling from my need.

Booby-trapped by a hole
in a rotted plank,
which splintered into shards
I tumbled
into a pile of stinking seaweed
beneath the boardwalk.

I often dream about what-if. What if I had been less shy, or if my mother had been warm and caring, what if I had been secure enough to ask for help, what if she led a parent revolt and had the teacher fired right away or had me taken out of her class. And, what if Mom had hugged me. In my what-if dream I would have known that I was intelligent and able and worthwhile.

Hurt

The lioness was limping
a fierce hunter, she was
not used to going slowly
or feeling vulnerable.

In her lair she licked
her wound and tried
to ignore her hunger,
even the frailest antelope
outran her today.
She roared her displeasure
then slept.

A few days later she could hunt,
but couldn't understand
her new hesitancy, her stomach
was full but her ferocity was gone
her anticipation of an exciting kill
was replaced with dread.

When I was ten years old my mother was diagnosed with breast cancer and she was in and out of the hospital for surgery and radiation treatments for the next four years until she died when I was in eighth grade. The three of us raised ourselves even more so after that.

My mother wasn't a complainer even when she had cancer. She taught me that whatever comes along, you just deal with it. My mother, in spite of what must have been a frightening disease just found ways of doing things without making a fuss.

I guess I didn't think much of the operations and hospital because she didn't, she went away, making sure everything at home was set up for however long she thought it would be, and then came home again. No big deal. It was just something she did. No anger, no tears, no shouting or cursing the fates, just make do if you can, by yourself, if not, with as little disruption as possible. I guess my parents thought that it was better not to discuss things with kids. Or maybe they didn't discuss them at all.

When my mother was in the hospital she wanted to see us, but no children were allowed. My dad said the rule was stupid and found a way. There was a large iron fire escape up the outside of the hospital. It ended at a window in the solarium located at the end of the hospital corridor. He led us to the stairs and said to wait outside until we saw him in the window four floors up.

Clutching my little sister's hand and climbing one handed up the fire escape stairway to my father was terrifying. I knew we were going to see my mother who was in the hospital again. I wanted to see her, but even more, I wanted her to come home, to be home, I missed her. I clutched the railing with my free hand, not letting go until I was securely on the next step. I was sure I was going to trip and fall and drag my sister down with me. My legs, used to running around the neighborhood, and pedaling my bike for hours on end, were fighting every step. I felt clumsy and unsteady. Marion, holding my hand without a worry, scampered up the stairs next to me and giggled, as I lifted her up to my dad. Climbing in through the window was a huge relief, but I wasn't ready for what I was about to see.

We snuck down the hallway to the third room from the end, and my dad closed the door. We ran over to a really high bed with one end raised up, where my mother was sitting. I was excited to see her, but everything was strange. I didn't know what to say, she was Mom, but she wasn't. She was very pale and had tubes on her arms. My sister bounded up on the bed and snuggled up for a hug and a kiss. She chatted away about what happened in school and about the big stairs she just climbed. I stood there twisting my hands together, feeling like a stranger and didn't say a word. After a while Mom called me over and asked how things were at home, how I was doing at school. I mumbled a few monosyllables, the words sticking in my throat. All I wanted to know was when she would be coming home.

We did this many, many times. Later my dad told us that once the solarium was being used as a room because the hospital was crowded and the old man patient complained to the staff that there were children running in and out of his room, they scoffed at him and shushed him with sleeping pills.

Even in the hospital room as sick as she was, my mom continued to tell me what to buy at the market and what to make for dinner.

I ached for attention; I lapped it up in any form, and made up lies just so my mother would notice me. One summer afternoon after a really energetic game of some kind I was flushed and sweaty I ran home and told my mother I was sick with a fever so she would put me to bed and tend to me.

Another time I told my mother that the teacher allowed my classmate Robert to do something that she didn't allow me to do, I was looking for sympathy, maybe a hug and some commiseration but it backfired as she marched me to the school and confronted the teacher and they found out I was lying, I was embarrassed and also punished.

I remember sitting in the bathroom on the toilet lid helping as my mother slowly dressed, after I fastened her bra and stuffed the cups with hankies I pulled her dress around her arm; it was a button-front blue checked cotton housedress.

I no longer reacted to the ugly wounds the discolored scars, which slashed across her chest, where her breasts used to be. We discussed what to have for dinner and what we had to do to get it ready, I was almost a teenager and as the oldest girl, my mother was making sure I knew how to keep house, she knew why, I just thought she was teaching me how to help her.

As an almost teen with budding breasts, seeing my mother this way was traumatizing in and of itself, and because my mother never discussed what she was going through with me there was nothing to help me process the impact of seeing what could easily be described as a mutilation. I, as my mother did, learned to accept the unacceptable, swallow my feelings and carry on.

I have no memory of being told that things I did were terrific or super or wonderful. If it came out good, it was the way it was supposed to be. My mother paid a lot of attention to how to do things, but none at all to how I was feeling. I had no idea how to love never having received any indication of it from either parent, or even witnessed it between them.

I was never warned that the cancer was not far from killing her, I had no clue it would be fatal, just that it made her sick and I wanted her to get better. Everyone I ever knew who got sick got better. I had had chicken pox, measles, and mumps, and as nasty as they were, I got better, and I fully expected the same for my mother.

Mom never told me how she felt, or if she was scared, or that she would miss us. She didn't prepare us emotionally in any way, but then she never had. A sick mother doesn't have much energy for supervising children, so the very little we had anyway dwindled to none.

When I was around eleven, one of the neighbor women told me to go home and wash my hair and brush my teeth which were green with scum from lack of brushing. That is how neglected my sister and I were. I ran home and took a bath; I washed my hair with soap in the dirty bath water. It must not have been too bad as the neighbor told me I looked much better.

With everything going on at home, having to take care of myself and later being enrolled in my mother's homemaking "class" I didn't have much leftover for school work, nothing much could sink in with so much else going in inside my head anyway. I hated school with a passion and because I knew I was not as smart as the other kids, I all but gave up. I did enough to pass so I wouldn't be held back.

I recently tried to remember Christmases at home while my mom was sick and afterward. I drew a blank, I do not remember a one, or birthdays, or my entire grades 8 and 9. I have completely buried many, too painful, memories.

Thinking back to what I did remember, I time travelled and was there, in the past, and I was that little kid reliving the feeling of being confused all the time, of being the only one in school who was different and didn't know what was going on. I do very much <u>not</u> like the powerlessness and being alone. My mind resisted being back there; the negative feelings were intense and physical with a big dose of fear.

The thought of sitting in a classroom in my little wooden desk, and the feeling of coming up short in what was expected of me and feeling guilty was strong and very real. The memories also bring back the feelings. No wonder I buried myself in books, at least they made sense, and were an escape. No wonder I shoved uncomfortable feelings way down deep.

What a horrible way to feel all the time with no way to know why or even that help was needed. Did I think this was normal? I knew I was different, I was sure I was stupid in everything except reading. What a hell of a way to have a childhood. I didn't blame my parents, only myself.

Early Frost

The night winds
hadn't received the memo about Spring.
Pollen dust tarnished frosting puddles,
tears from emerging buds
that slowly shriveled while waiting
for the miracle of morning.

Tightly clustered groves
disdained the attacking drafts
they stood together
weathering the onslaught,
their inner core protected
by shared warmth.

The solitary sapling's icy blossoms
were fresh snow littering the ground,
deftly disguising
the crippling damage.

The School psychologist gave me a test; I had to define words, the only one I didn't know was "edifice" (I said it was an eagle's nest). I turned red and he made a big deal about my being embarrassed about not knowing only one word when I knew all the others, I couldn't escape from him soon enough. I thought he was criticizing me for being embarrassed but now I am sure he was trying to praise me.

My mother was there and not there. I mean that when she was well, she did the housewife things, my father made a good salary so she had help with cleaning and ironing. But she was not someone who played with her kids. She was a presence, but not a warm loving person.

I was the middle kid, and I am sure that had something to do with the lack of attention, but my mother had a warped idea of what it was to be a mother, and didn't think kids needed anything but food and clothes. I was left to raise myself, to figure out how the world worked all by myself.

Middle

A gully washer, the neighbor
sitting next to me said,
a real gully washer.

The street was a river
of broken branches
and orphan shoes.

Sheltering on the porch I watched
the plights of three lively bobbing
logs along the curb.

The biggest surged ahead
and spilled headlong into a sewer.
 The littlest spun off
into a dead ended eddy.

The middle one smashed into
the curb, went under and
rose to the top again and again
each time losing a little headway
and a little more bark.

I got to my feet jumping
and cheering it on.
I ran along the sidewalk getting
soaked, running to keep up with the
feisty fighter shouting at it to be careful,
to hang on, to watch out, to please survive.

And then came the day she went away and didn't come back.

My dad said. "I need you." And off to the funeral parlor we went. Dad had been crying or silent ever since Mom died, and now he said I had to help him with the arrangements. I had never even been to a funeral and here, at fourteen, I was on my way to what? I had no idea. I wanted to ask, but I couldn't make him listen. I was a wreck but didn't show it. I didn't know how to feel or act, so I swallowed everything and just waited. We walked into a room with red velvet wallpaper and a dark red soft carpet. My father sat sobbing in a red velvet chair off to the side of a soft man in a black suit who was sitting at a dark wood desk. I was front and center. I was peppered with questions - which style casket, which bible verses should be read, which hymns did I want played and what flowers would I want on the casket?

I stammered, "She has to have wild pink roses."

The black suit, with an eyebrow lifted, gave a sneer of a glance and said he didn't know where to find wild roses. He urged me to approve the ones in the picture under the plastic sleeve in the funeral book.

"No!" I said, "I don't know where either, but she has to have pink roses, she loved wild pink roses".

"I hardly think it matters now", the suit said.

I sat stock still, my fingers tightly gripped the edges of the chair as I stubbornly replied, "Of course it matters, she only likes wild roses".

I evaded into a memory. My mother and I were in our back yard by our shingle garage covered with wild pink roses. Our scissors snipped, and we danced armfuls of sweet prickly boughs into the house and to vases in every room, giddy from the spicy aroma.

A rude "Ahem" brought me back. I decided my mother wouldn't want me to argue with this stupid man, so I said, "Those are fine", pointing to his awful book, "But make sure they are pink." I wasn't going to fully give in.

What in hell were the adults in my life thinking when they allowed my father to put this responsibility on my head? Where was my grandmother, my aunt, or even my nineteen year old brother? I had not shed a tear yet, not when I was told she died and not during this ordeal of shepherding my father from mortuary to lawyer, to church.

Not even the minister questioned that I was in charge, this skinny little dead-eyed stoic shell shocked kid was in charge, and not one adult thought it was strange and that just maybe, possibly it might not be good for a kid to have this responsibility.

I sat all through the funeral without a tear; I shook hands afterward with all the mourners without mourning myself. I thanked everyone in my father's stead like the perfect grownup I wasn't.

After my mother died, I was, as a teenager, a bizarre mix of needy, ashamed, people pleaser, defect hider, and procrastinator. I was sure that everyone else had things all worked out and only I was a confused mess, so I kept everything inside, I couldn't let anyone know what a screwup I was. I had to go through what every teen goes through with the added handicap of having no parents to support or even discipline me.

I now understand that what my father expected of me was impossible for a kid my age to live up to, but at the time I felt horribly guilty that I couldn't handle the cooking, cleaning and laundry that my mother so carefully taught me to do, and school, so I gave up.

I was emotionally unprepared for the trauma of my mother's death, I hadn't been warned that she might not get better and her sudden, to me, death was a shock. To make things worse my father ignored my sister's, brother's and my feelings. My sister escaped to her friend's house, my brother disappeared and I, instead of being comforted and counselled was expected to become an instant adult, that feeling of failure was everlasting.

Because of that feeling that I had failed, what I was going through at home during the time after my mother died and when I escaped into marriage is still, even after a lot of therapy, very hard to reveal. I never revealed anything much of me to anyone, and especially the disaster that was those days.

My father was useless, completely useless, and more than that, he was damaging as he let everything go to hell and did nothing about it. I was supposed to be the one to keep house, that the house was a dirty mess was guilt that I shouldered but did nothing about. I knew I should be home cleaning and doing laundry but I didn't want to, I wanted to go to the sweet shop with my friends, and I wanted to ride my friend's horse and hang around the barn, and I wanted to be a teenager, not a housewife.

So I lived in a pig sty, which at one point became overrun with roaches, which must have come in on some grocery boxes. Coming into the kitchen in the morning and seeing the bugs in the sink gave me a lifelong loathing. My father continued to ignore everything.

Needless to say we had no rules or regulations, I was in my teen years and had absolutely no one to tell me what I should or shouldn't do. Once, when a group of my friends and I were in the park after dinner, someone said they had to be home by eight o'clock or their mother would give them hell, I lied and said, "Yeah, me too, I have to be home by eight also". It felt good to think that someone would care about me enough to give me a curfew, but no one did. So I muddled through. When I think about me then I cry for that confused little kid.

Thinking about my mother's death, even now, is very confusing. I should have been wracked with the loss of the most important person in my life. But I wasn't. She knew she was going to die, so did she talk to me, and prepare me emotionally? No. Did she help me learn how to take care of my little sister? No. What did she do? She taught me how to cook, and how to sew. How to plan meals, how to shop, but not once did she tell me she was going to die, or tell me how she was feeling, just how to use the pressure cooker. When she did die, did I lose my mother, no I don't think so, I lost a tutor, a housekeeper, a robot.

Who Cares

Every cage was wrapped in blankets
on a frigid Florida winter night.
The Wildlife Center's wounded
needed protection.

Now the day was warming
so I unwrapped the cages,
and folded the odds and ends
of donated blankets.

One had pink elephants on it,
what could that mean?

One folded back
into a bag maybe a beach tote.

The one on the bobolink cage
was a baby blankie with chewed
and sucked on corners.

Caring people wrapped the cages
in blankets donated
by other caring people.

Caring people wrap others in warmth
and love, they care about animals and kids
and family and they wrap and hug
and, they, don't, leave.

No wonder I couldn't cry at the funeral, no wonder I wondered why I wasn't sadder. I saw my father sobbing all the time and wondered why I wasn't. I stayed in my room and read, I want over to Gail's house and rode her horse, and tried to be away from home as often as I could.

I avoided my father as much as I could. He was tight, and I had to wheedle money for clothes and things I needed. He always acted surprised that I needed anything.

I really wondered what was wrong with me. Well, I was what I was raised to be, as much as I was raised at all. I was a sucker for any one at all who showed me the least little bit of affection or attention, I craved attention, I craved approval; I hated home and couldn't wait to leave.

Poor mixed up teenager. I hung around with the kids who were kind of wild, but smoking, drinking beer, cutting school and dancing to the juke box was the worst we could think up to do, I was ten years too early to have access to any serious damage. I wonder if I would have done drugs, maybe - probably. I learned as a tiny girl to stop expecting. Over and over my hopes were unfulfilled, so I didn't hope, I flattened out my reactions.

Worry

There's a lion eating my foot
he won't stop, he says it's a dog
eat dog world, so don't worry.

But I am worrying, it's my foot
and I need it, so I ask him again to stop
I think he is laughing, it's hard to tell
because he has a mouth full of my foot
and his words are kind of garbled
and he is blowing bloody bubbles.

I am getting a little concerned
maybe I should start running away
but I only have one and a half feet
so running could be a little hard
and he would probably catch up
and be mad I took his dinner
and maybe want to eat my other foot
and then I would be really screwed.
So, I don't run, I stay.

What helped me was that I lived in books, I learned about the world from books; that was what was real to me. My life outside of books was a roller coaster of emotions all inside my head, and never expressed. I was like a rotating radar dish, checking the landscape and the dangers around and reacting to minimize any threat.

You know about PTSD the condition that affects war veterans and survivors of car accidents, natural disasters, and isolated acts of violence. What was happening to me was Complex PTSD similar to but distinct from PTSD. C-PTSD is defined as severe, repetitive trauma that typically happens in childhood involving sustained abuse or abandonment (neglect) by a caregiver. On the surface, it may seem as if PTSD and Complex PTSD are alike – they both happen as the result of something deeply traumatic; they cause flashbacks, nightmares, and insomnia; and, they can make people live in fear even when they are safe. But the very heart and center of C-PTSD is considerably different because of the continued ongoing trauma that causes it. It distorts a child's perceptions and causes lifelong repercussions. It reshapes a child's entire mind and outlook on life.

No wonder at fifteen I welcomed the attention of a seventeen year old boy who lavished praise on my looks and didn't care about school work. We spent every free moment together. I didn't say a word when he refused to allow me to hang out with my friends. I just tossed them aside. He was isolating me for his purposes, not mine, but who knew? I agreed to marry him and got engaged on my high school graduation day. My father was just glad to have someone to take me over. I was just glad to get out of that loveless house, and away from the mess. We were married when I was nineteen and he was twenty one.

On my wedding day I had second thoughts, I was pretty sure I shouldn't be doing this, but the dress was paid for, the church booked and the reception hall rented. I didn't have the guts to back down; I made myself go through with it.

That same, something's wrong, feeling stayed with me through my entire marriage, until I finally acted on it. It took 29 years.

Love, I had no idea what that was, but I was swept up into marriage, we were playing house. That's when I became a neat freak, in reaction to the mess of a house I left. We talked about things, not feelings or issues. He was the boss; I was content to be with a person who "cared". My neediness was being fed. I no longer had to be ashamed to invite anyone into my house.

Perfectly

They're just jeans, mid rise
boot cut faded denim.
They sit perfectly a bit below my hips
and make my butt look better
than I dreamed.
The straight leg bottoms hide
part of my feet and make them look
smaller, skinny jeans don't do that.
I quickly grab them from the dryer
and open the ironing board.
They're too long to fit
so I iron the legs first
and then the tops.
The creases must be sharp and straight
and I iron them over and over and over.

I had two children, a big house and a husband which takes up a lot of time which left no time for me, but I was slowly learning some things. I learned that I was the idea of a wife to my husband; not a real person, as long as I was pretty and thin, and kept the house clean and the kids out of the way things were fine. As long as everything was done and dinner was on the table on time, I could do pretty much what I wanted, only appearances mattered to him.

He harassed and insulted me until I lost the baby weight. I learned not to fight with him, I was totally unable to handle confrontation and unable to stand up for myself. He fought so mean and dirty that I dissolved into angry tears and ran. Again traumatized, I quickly learned how to keep everything the way he wanted. I shoved my feelings deeper and deeper inside along with my anger and did not allow it to surface.

We had a neighbor who was a retired accountant; he badgered me into going to college. I knew I wasn't smart enough to go to college, but he convinced me to take the entrance test, I passed, I took an evening class, I passed, I kept going, my confidence grew.

Steel

The sprinkling system
covered wide swaths,
semi-circles guaranteed
to keep the grass green
and the pansies smiling.

Neglected in the arid
wedge between two
overlaps was a miniature
face.

I stroked its tiny
purple cheeks, their softness
belying its courage.

Looking back I amaze myself at what I did. While not disrupting my husband's life at all, (my mother in law helped baby sit) I substitute taught while going to college at night. I graduated magna cum laude.

Just after graduation I got a job in the Public School. That confused inadequate kid still lived inside me, but people seemed to think I was good at what I did. Along the way I got a masters' in Counseling and Special Services and was certified as a reading specialist and I earned another masters' in public school administration.

Difficulty with self-perception is another fundamental struggle for C-PSTD survivors whose identity development was so fiercely interrupted. In its simplest form, how they see themselves versus how the world perceives them is shockingly different. Some may feel they embody nothing but shame and that they are "bad". Others believe themselves to be fundamentally helpless; they were let down by so many who could've stopped their abuse but didn't, so it "must just be them". Many see themselves as responsible for what happened to them and thus unworthy of kindness or love because "they did this to themselves". Others worry they are always in the way or an unforgivable burden. Startling enough, all of these feelings and more can live inside someone who, to you, seems like the most brilliant, competent, strong, and compassionate human being.

After some years I was transferred to the middle school. I only lasted four years, the students I taught were so emotionally needy that I was wearing myself out defending and helping them. It was impossible for me to remain detached, I knew I should but couldn't. These kids were the same age I was when my mother died. I empathized through "love" affairs, refereed spats and was a go-to person for every crisis, panic and lost lunch money. I often couldn't sleep worrying about them.

Awwww!

My favorites' are the clever dear kitten ones,
where the blasé tom relates
cat lore to the little ginger tabby.

No matter how many times I watch the calico
survive a cucumber attack with hissing leaps
I also jump.

The one where the cute kid tries to dunk
the cat in the pool
and winds up the wet one is a hoot.

Click the mouse and the cats perform,
they don't care how late at night it is.

A nice thing about that age is a few years later some of them told me how much I helped them; the little ones couldn't do that. But the little ones didn't chew hunks out of my hide either.

I was elected to the Teachers' Association board where I was head of the negotiating team and then was elected president. I was asked to become an administrator. Every promotion and added responsibility validated my non-dumbness, a surprise but it felt good. I didn't say no.

I filled time with my kids, teaching school and friends. My husband and I still talked only about things, mostly the kids and his jobs. I had many friends but never allowed any to get too close.

As the years passed my husband got more and more verbally abusive, nothing I did was good enough, I was too fat, my clothes were too dowdy and school-teacherish.

I was miserable; we tried couples therapy which led to my first divorce. I saw the therapist a few times after that but I was so sensitive about my past and my feelings that I would never freely open up to her, and she was not perceptive enough to understand what I needed so I stopped seeing her. I wish I had realized this and tried to find help somewhere else. I wish I had found Ira at that time as my life would have been so much easier.

Picking partners, apparently, is not my strength, after the divorce I met and married Jim. We were good for each other because we were both teachers and just free of domineering spouses. We were having fun. We retired and travelled all over the world.

A Poem About Villas in Italy Because They Made Me Cry

The tri-states Mom called them,
she'd never been beyond.

A horror that I also might die without ever visiting
villas perched on the cliffs of Capri,
defying sanity and gravity, grotto boats specks
below,
or colossal sand dunes topped by tombs of ancients,
seared a longing into my young awareness.

Life intervened,
yellowed, fingered and tattered brochures
piled deep in my bedside basket.

This gray haired child,
sniffling into a tissue at a café table
in the Piazza Umberto
sends a salute skyward.

Jim and I were also a disaster together as he withdrew into a bottle more and more and I with my usual aversion to confrontation drew away and went off on my own, doing things that interested me. It worked until it didn't, and I wound up in Ira's office.

Sweet White Flowers

"Promise me that or nothing at all"
Maya Angelou said to me
this night when I am reading poems
instead of writing them.

I don't want her paradise
but I do like that phrase.
What it means to me
is on the tip of my tongue.
I know
 "Promise me that or nothing at all"
is tremendously significant
but I can't think why.

Outside my window the lime tree
is putting out tiny new green leaves
its flowers are marvelously sweet,
not, sweet ride dude, sweet
but the sweet of brownies
baking in the oven
and the sweet of baby
powder, sweet.

Every year the old tree
does its job, it survives
summer storms and heat
and sap slowing winter
it bends and sometimes breaks
but there they are again
tiny new green leaves
and sweet white flowers.
Promise me that,
or nothing.

I better understand how neglect in my childhood shaped everything I did and do including my unfortunate choices of men. I now have enough understanding to move out of the quicksand. I recognize how I coped all my life – I chose overachievement, it was really frenetic achievement, and not drug addiction but it could have gone that way. I feel much better about the future. I have some very hard work and a lot of unlearning to do, but for the first time I am optimistic and looking forward to learning what it is to be happy.

Healing

Her tongue felt rough
on the numb ragged scar.
Crouching against the far wall
of the lair she finally shut her eyes
but her ears stayed up and aware.
Sleeping soundly, her legs twitched.

Muscles rippling
and head held high
bounding effortlessly
through the long brown grass
she leaped,
her long lethal claws
downed and gutted
her prey.

Startled awake
by a nearby purring cough
a deep yearning
dulled her fear
and she limped out.

- *Being ignored causes the same chemical reaction in the brain as experiencing a physical injury.*

- *The kids who need the most love will ask for it in the most unloving of ways.*

- *"Attention Deficit Disorder" should be called "Attention to lots & lots & lots of things & and some other stuff except the one thing I should be really paying attention to disorder."*

- *Our children pick up a great deal from how we embrace them each morning, how we react when they break our favorite vase, how we handle ourselves in a traffic accident, how we sit and talk to them, whether we really look at what they show us, and whether we take an interest in what they say.*

- *You cannot heal a lifetime of pain overnight, be patient with yourself, it takes as long as it takes to rebuild yourself.*

- *Sometimes we survive by forgetting.*

- *Courage is not the absence of fear, but rather the judgment that something else is more important than fear.*

- *Safety is of the utmost importance for healing of childhood complex trauma, every time the adult survivor faces something that feels unsafe, fear, anxiety and emotional flashbacks can occur.*

- *"Survivors of any and all abuse become very good at anticipating the moods of others, looks, actions, all of it in an effort to survive. Believing that if we can't be agreeable, be compliant and loving, do things how they want, and that we will be safe. This becomes our way of life.* Darlene Ouimet

- *Your ability to relax is in direct proportion to your ability to trust life.*

- *You never need to apologize for how you choose to survive.*

- *PTSD: It's not that the person is refusing to let go of the past, but the past is refusing to let go of the person.*

25963350R00033

Printed in Great Britain
by Amazon